WATER INSECTS

WATER INSECTS

by Sylvia A. Johnson

Photographs by Modoki Masuda

A Lerner Natural Science Book

Lerner Publications Company ▪ Minneapolis

595.7092
J

Sylvia A. Johnson, Series Editor

Translation of original text by Wesley M. Jacobsen

The publisher wishes to thank Jerry W. Heaps, Registered Professional Entomologist, for his assistance in the preparation of this book.

Additional photographs by: pp. 5, 7, Independent Picture Service; p. 34 (lower left), Hidekazu Kubo.

The glossary on page 46 gives definitions and pronunciations of words shown in **bold type** in the text. On page 47 is a list of the scientific and common names of the water insects discussed in the book.

LIBRARY OF CONGRESS CATALOGING-IN-PUBLICATION DATA

Johnson, Sylvia A.
  Water insects / by Sylvia A. Johnson ; photographs by Modoki Masuda.
    p. cm. — (A Lerner natural science book)
  Adaptation of: Suisei konchū no himitsu.
  Includes index.
  Summary: Describes the physical characteristics, behavior, and life cycles of some insects that spend most of their lives in the water.
  ISBN: 0-8225-1489-3 (lib bdg.)
  1. Insects, Aquatic — Juvenile literature. [1. Insects, Aquatic.] I. Masuda, Modoki, ill. II. Masuda, Modoki. Suisei konchū no himitsu. III. Title. IV. Series.
QL467.2.J64 1989
595.7092 — dc20   89-12372
                                                    CIP
                                                    AC

International Standard Book Number: 0-8225-1489-3
Library of Congress Catalog Number: 89-12372

1 2 3 4 5 6 7 8 9 10 98 97 96 95 94 93 92 91 90 89

The backswimmer is one of the strange and fascinating insects that live in the water.

Everyone has admired graceful flying insects like butterflies or watched colorful ladybugs creeping over garden plants. But there are some other common insects that you may have never seen. These insects spend most of their lives in the waters of ponds and streams.

Water insects are as much at home in the water as their relatives are in the air or on the ground. Skillful swimmers and divers, they breathe, eat, and even produce their young in a watery environment.

Quiet bodies of water like this pond provide a home for many kinds of insects.

AT HOME IN THE WATER

What kinds of insects would you find if you waded into a pond with a collecting net? You might come back with a assortment of very different animals.

Some insects spend only a part of their lives in the water. Dragonflies, for example, go through their early development in ponds and streams. When a dragonfly hatches from its egg, its body is not completely developed. Until its wings and other body parts grow, the young dragonfly lives in the water, breathing through gills. When its development is complete, the insect emerges from the water and flies away.

Other insects spend almost all the stages of their lives in or on the water. These are the true water insects. Although most of them have wings and can fly, they do not often take to the air. Instead, they get around by paddling, swimming, and diving. Some can even walk on the water's surface.

After this immature dragonfly completes its development, it will leave the water and live on land.

A giant water bug killing a tadpole

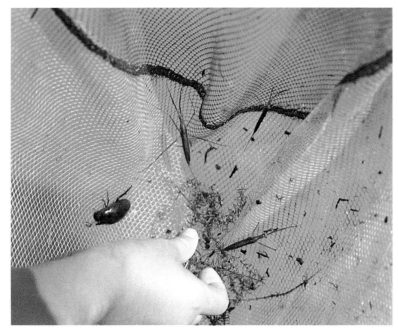

This collection net holds several kinds of water insects, including a large water scavenger beetle (left) and three of the bugs known as water scorpions (center).

BEETLES AND BUGS

The most common water insects belong to two large groups, or orders, in the class of insects. One group is made up of beetles. The members of the other group are bugs.

On land or in the water, beetles are very common insects. There are more than 300,000 different species, or kinds, of beetles throughout the world. The spotted ladybug in your garden is a beetle, despite its name. So is the firefly whose flashing light can sometimes be seen on summer nights.

Whether they fly through the air or swim in the water, all beetles have certain features in common. Their front wings,

Both of these insects are beetles. The predaceous diving beetle (left) lives in the water, while the cockchafer (right) is a land beetle. Both have the hard, smooth front wings that are typical of all beetles.

which are hard and shell-like, serve as covers for their filmy hind wings. (The scientific name for the order of beetles is Coleoptera, which means "sheath-wing.") Beetles have mouthparts designed for chewing food. And all beetles go through four different stages of development as they become adults.

"Bug" is the name that many people use for all kinds of insects, especially the creeping, crawling ones. Scientists use the term to refer to only one order of insects—Hemiptera, the true bugs.

Just like beetles, many kinds of bugs live on land. The bed bug is one of the best known of the land-dwelling bugs. Stink

The giant water bug (right) and the stink bug (above) are both true bugs, members of the order Hemiptera. A land-dwelling insect, the stink bug produces an unpleasant odor that discourages predators.

bugs and chinch bugs are also members of the group. Many insects that have "bug" as part of their common names are not true bugs. The potato bug is one of these "false" bugs. Like the ladybug, it is actually a beetle.

True bugs, like beetles, have distinctive wings that have earned them their scientific name. Hemiptera means "half-wing." The word refers to the insects' front wings, which have leathery bases and filmy outer edges. A bug's mouthparts are not used for chewing but for piercing and sucking out fluid. Finally, true bugs develop in a different way than beetles, going through only three stages on their way to becoming adults.

The surface of this pond is dotted with the bugs known as water striders or pond skaters.

INSECTS ON TOP OF THE WATER

Whether they are beetles or bugs, all water insects live in a similar kind of environment. They also have the same basic needs. But the insects have found many different ways to make use of their surroundings and to satisfy their needs.

Some water insects spend most of their time on or near the surface of the water. Here they find air to breathe and the food they need to survive. Surface insects include both beetles and bugs.

Take a close look at a quiet pond, and you may see hundreds of little whirligig beetles swimming rapidly over the surface. This insect's common name comes from the whirling, circular path it makes on the water.

The whirligig beetle (right) has two pairs of eyes, one pair located on the upper part of its head and one on the lower part. This unusual arrangement allows the beetle to look for **prey** both on the surface of the pond and under the water.

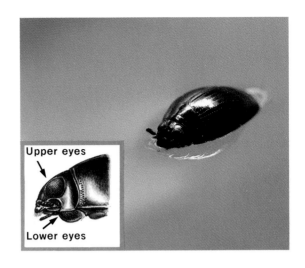

Upper eyes

Lower eyes

The backswimmer (below) is a bug that spends most of its time just under the water's surface. This strange insect swims on its back, using its hairy hind legs to row itself along. Its torpedo-shaped body helps it to move quietly when hunting prey. The backswimmer attacks animals on the water's surface. When an insect or a tadpole drifts by, the bug reaches up and grabs it with its strong front legs.

In this photograph, you are looking at a backswimmer from under the water. The real insect is on the bottom, while the top image is a reflection seen on the underside of the water surface. Another picture of a backswimmer appears on page 5.

13

A water strider's legs make small dents in the surface film of the water (left). The oily hairs on the ends of its legs (above) repel water and also trap air that helps to keep the bug afloat.

The bug known as the water strider can often be seen "walking" on the surface of ponds. It uses its short front legs to catch insects that have fallen on the water. Its other two pairs of legs support it and move it over the water's surface.

The water strider's ability to walk on water depends on **surface tension**, a characteristic of water and other liquids. Surface tension is a force that causes water to behave as if a thin, elastic film covered its surface. It is produced by the attraction of water molecules to each other.

The "film" created by surface tension can support a water strider because its body is very light. The insect's long legs spread its weight over a large area, further reducing the pressure on the surface. The ends of a water strider's legs are covered with hairs that are coated with an oily secretion. This oil repels water and helps to keep the bug afloat.

Above: Water striders gather around an injured dragonfly that has fallen on the water surface. The bugs will kill the dragonfly and suck out its body fluids. *Right:* Another small predator that can walk on water is the fishing spider. Like the water strider, it has hairs on its legs that repel water.

15

Left: Water scorpions have hook-like front legs (below) that they use to hold prey. Like all true bugs, their mouthparts (above) are designed to pierce and to suck out fluids. *Right:* The long tube at the end of a water scorpion's abdomen is used in breathing.

INSECTS UNDER THE WATER

While the water strider skates around on the pond's surface, other insects are lurking under the water. Here they find the animals they depend on for food. Some of these insects wait quietly for their prey. They hide in ambush under floating leaves or among the plants on the pond bottom. These hunters include bugs like the water scorpion and the giant water bug.

The water scorpion gets its common name from the long, thin tube at the end of its body, which looks something like the tail of the poisonous land scorpion. Water scorpions feed on tadpoles, insects, and other prey, seizing them with their hook-like front legs.

16

The giant water bug (above) is also equipped with hooked front legs. This large insect, which can be as much as two inches (about five centimeters) in length, is able to catch frogs and fish as well as smaller creatures. Both bugs get their nourishment by piercing the bodies of their prey and sucking out fluids.

Water scavenger beetles often hide among water plants during the day (above) and become active at night. They usually feed on dead plants (left), performing a clean-up service for the pond community.

Other underwater insects are active hunters. They swim around, searching for a likely meal. Some of these insects feed on animals, while others eat plant material.

Predaceous diving beetles are probably the fiercest of the underwater predators. These streamlined insects are expert swimmers and divers. They will attack almost anything in the water, fish as well as other insects. Their powerful chewing mouthparts can devour most of a fish's body, leaving only the bones. Diving beetles will also eat dead animals.

The water scavenger beetle has the same streamlined appearance as the diving beetle, but it is not as good a swimmer. It paddles around slowly in the water, looking for dead plants on which to feed. Some water scavenger beetles will also eat meat.

Two different kinds of predaceous diving beetles eating a fish. The word *predaceous* means "living by preying on other animals," which is a very good description of these water beetles. All members of the family Dysticidae, they range in size from less than ⅛ inch (about 3 millimeters) to almost 2 inches (about 5 centimeters) in length. No matter what their size, predaceous diving beetles are strong and skillful hunters.

In swimming, a diving beetle strokes with both hind legs at the same time. When the legs are pushing back against the water, as in this photograph, the long hairs stand out. When the legs move forward, the hairs lie flat, cutting down resistance to the water.

The predaceous diving beetle is one of the best swimmers in the insect world. Its smooth flat body glides through the water with great ease. Diving beetles have powerful hind legs shaped like paddles. These legs are fringed with long, thick hairs, which increases their resistance to the water.

When a diving beetle swims, it tucks its four front legs into grooves on its body (above). This makes its shape even more streamlined. The beetle pushes itself through the water with its hairy hind legs. A diving beetle's specialized legs are very useful for swimming but not much good for walking. If the insect leaves the water, it depends on its strong wings to provide transportation.

These photographs show the hind legs of different water insects. Those insects that swim under the water, like the water scavenger beetle (1) and the diving beetle (2), have the longest, thickest hair on their legs. The other insects shown usually stay on the surface or wait in ambush instead of swimming after prey. These insects—the backswimmer (3), the giant water bug (4), and the water scorpion (5)—have less hair on their legs.

Left: A water scavenger beetle sticks its head and upper body out of the water in order to take in air. *Right:* This view from below shows the silvery film of air on the abdomen of a water scavenger beetle.

BREATHING IN THE WATER

In order to survive in their watery world, water insects must have oxygen to breathe. Most of these insects cannot take oxygen from the water as fish do. They do not have gills like fish or like the immature dragonflies that live in water. Instead, their respiratory systems are like those of land insects, consisting of external openings called **spiracles** connected to a system of tubes.

In order to breathe underwater, most water insects get air from the surface. Some store a supply of air in special places on their bodies. Diving beetles and water scavenger beetles carry a bubble of air between their hard front wings and their backs. These insects may also collect air on the fine hairs that cover their abdomens. This thin film of air, called a **plastron**, often gives a silvery shine to the beetles' bodies.

A predaceous diving beetle comes to the surface to renew its air supply. Depending on conditions in the pond, the beetle can stay underwater from 2 to 10 minutes on the air that it takes in at one surfacing.

To renew its air supply, a diving beetle sticks the tip of its abdomen out of the water. The water scavenger beetle comes out head first when it needs more air.

A giant water bug extends the respiratory tubes at the end of its abdomen to take in air from the surface.

Instead of carrying a supply of air, other water insects use the "snorkel" system to get the oxygen they need. They take in air through **respiratory tubes** that they extend out of the water.

Giant water bugs have short respiratory tubes at the ends of their abdomens. The bugs extend their tubes only when they are taking in air. At other times, the tubes are pulled back inside their bodies.

Water scorpions have long respiratory tubes that cannot be withdrawn. These tubes are made up of two separate sections joined together. They are constructed in such a way that water cannot get into them when the insects are underwater.

Above: This water scorpion, which belongs to the genus *Ranatra*, has a respiratory tube almost as long as its body. *Right:* Two water scorpions mating. The members of this genus (*Laccotrepes*) have broader, shorter bodies and shorter tubes than their relative shown above.

Left: Water scorpions drying their wings in the sun. *Opposite:* A water scorpion in flight.

TAKING TO THE AIR

Although most water insects stay in or near the water, they sometimes spread their wings and fly. This may become necessary if their pond dries up or if food becomes scarce. Then they will have to find another place to live.

Diving beetles are powerful fliers. Like all beetles, they move only their hind wings when they fly, holding their hard front wings in one place. Giant water bugs are also good fliers. Both of these kinds of insects do most of their flying at night. You may sometimes see them gathered around electric lights near bodies of water.

Water scorpions and backswimmers are daytime fliers. With their light, thin bodies, many water scorpions are at home in the air. Before the insects can take off from the pond, however, they must spread out their wings and dry them.

Left: A female water scorpion laying her eggs in moss. *Above:* This giant water bug female (genus *Diplonychus*) is depositing her eggs on the back of her mate.

REPRODUCTION IN THE POND

When it comes time to lay eggs and produce young, it is not surprising that water insects stay close the water. Most of them, however, do not lay their eggs directly in the water. Female water scavenger beetles make egg cases out of a kind of silk and float them on the water's surface. They place their eggs in these floating cradles. Many kinds of water scorpions put their eggs in moss at the pond's edge or on sticks floating in the water.

Predaceous diving beetles and some kinds of giant water bugs attach their eggs to plants sticking up out of the water. Other kinds of giant water bugs put their eggs in a very unusual place. The female water bug sticks her eggs on the backs of the male bugs with whom she has mated.

Giant water bugs in the genus *Lethocerus* put their eggs on plants sticking out of the water. Here a female bug (bottom) is laying the eggs, while her mate keeps watch. This particular female produced a total of 96 eggs over a three-hour period.

Two giant water bug males (*Diplonychus*) raise themselves out of the pond to expose the eggs on their backs to the air.

Very few adult insects provide any care for their young after the eggs are laid, but there are a few exceptions. Social insects like bees, wasps, and termites guard and protect their eggs and young. Some water insects also care for their eggs.

When a female giant water bugs fastens her eggs to a male's back, the male is stuck with them until they hatch. He swims around with the eggs, sometimes raising them out of the water so that the young inside can get the air and warmth they need.

The giant water bug eggs that are attached to plants also receive protection. After the female lays the eggs, the male stays nearby to guard them. He may cover them with his body to hide them from predators. Sometimes he brings water from the pond in his mouth to moisten the eggs.

Right: A cluster of giant water bug eggs attached to a branch. *Above:* A male giant water bug (*Lethocerus*) uses his body to cover a cluster of eggs. He does this not only to protect the eggs from predators but also to keep them moist.

The photographs on these two pages show giant water bug nymphs (genus *Lethocerus*) emerging from their eggs. *Left:* The eggs begin to hatch about 10 days after they were laid. Their soft shells split open, and the heads of the nymphs appear. *Right:* About 10 minutes later, the nymphs are halfway out of their eggs.

THE EGGS HATCH

When bug eggs hatch, the young creatures that emerge look a lot like their parents. Their bodies are similar in shape, even though they are smaller and some parts are not completely developed. These immature bugs, known as **nymphs**, will not have to change much to become adults.

When beetle eggs hatch, the animals that emerge look nothing at all like adult beetles. These creatures, called **larvae**, are like the caterpillars that hatch from the eggs of butterflies. They are one of the four very different stages that butterflies, beetles, bees, and many other insects go through during their development. Bugs, like dragonflies and grasshoppers, have only three stages in their development.

32

Above: **Fifteen minutes after hatching began, the nymphs are almost completely emerged. They hang upside down from their shells, their front legs folded under their heads.** *Right:* **Hatching completed, the nymphs fall into the water of the pond. Their bodies are yellow now, but they will soon take on the color of adult giant water bugs.**

Above: After being carried on the male's back for about three weeks, giant water bug eggs (*Diplonychus*) begin to hatch.

Above: These water scorpion eggs (*Ranatra*) developed in damp moss for about two weeks before the nymphs emerged. The long rods extending from the eggs are respiratory tubes that help to bring air to the developing young.

Above: In this photograph, you can see the larva of a predaceous diving beetle emerging from an egg hidden inside the stem of a water plant. The egg was put into the stem by the mother beetle about two weeks earlier. *Right:* The larva of a water scavenger beetle emerges from its egg case three or four days after the egg was laid. As soon as it hatches, the larva will begin its life in the water, like all the larvae and nymphs shown here.

34

After developing for about three weeks, a water scorpion nymph (*Laccotrepes*) hatches from its egg. On the nymph's head is the end of the egg shell, with its long respiratory tubes. The heads of two other nymphs can be seen just emerging from their eggs.

One giant water bug nymph (left) eating another nymph. The first nymph is in an early stage of development, and its colors are very different from those of an adult.

THE YOUNG DEVELOP

Whether beetles or bugs, young water insects go through their early development in the water. Here the larvae and nymphs spend a large part of their time looking for food. Most eat meat at this stage of their lives even though they may be plant eaters as adults. The hungry young insects will even eat each other if nothing else is available.

While they are in the water, the developing insects get air in different ways. Some can take oxygen directly from the water at this stage of their lives. Other must come to the surface to breathe, just as they will do as adults.

Left: A giant water bug nymph in its second stage of development feeding on a tadpole. *Right:* The larva of a predaceous diving beetle (right) attacks a giant water bug nymph.

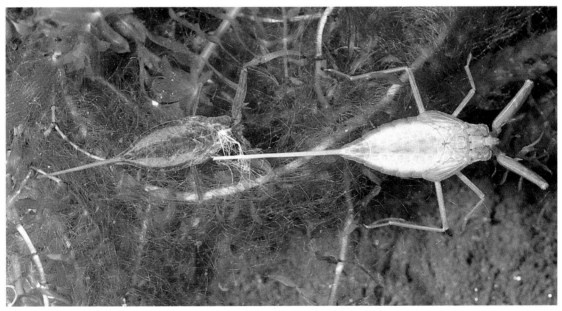

The nymphs and larvae of water insects grow through the process of molting, or shedding the outer coverings of their bodies. This water scorpion nymph (right) has just shed its old covering (left). The nymph is now in its final stage of development, and its adult wings have begun to grow.

Giant water bug nymphs (*Lethocerus*) molt five times before becoming adults. The nymph shown above is going through its first molt. On the right is a nymph after the fourth molt. It has almost all its adult body parts, but the wings are still undeveloped.

The developing water insects grow in size by **molting**, or shedding the outer layers of their bodies. The outer layer of an insect's body is called an **exoskeleton**. Like the internal skeleton of humans, it provides support and protection for the soft body parts. But the exoskeleton does not expand as the insect grows. It must be shed and replaced by a larger exoskeleton that develops underneath it. This is what happens when the insect molts.

Most water bugs molt four to five times as nymphs. Then their development is complete, and they become adults. The photographs on these two pages show a giant water bug nymph during the stages of its development.

These photographs show the fifth and final molt of a giant water bug nymph. In the small picture above, the adult insect is beginning to emerge from the old nymphal covering. The large photo above shows the adult bug just after emergence. Its body is soft and yellow in color, but it will soon become hard and brown (lower photo), like other members of its species.

Left: A diving beetle larva swimming in the water after its second molt. *Above:* After the larva molts for the third time, it leaves the water and makes a chamber in the dirt at the pond's edge.

The larvae of many water beetles also molt several times, each time growing larger. When their molts are complete, however, the larvae are not ready to become adults. First they must go through another stage of development.

A beetle larva must change into a **pupa** before it can become an adult. The photographs on these two pages show the larva of a predaceous diving beetle going through this remarkable change.

After spending several weeks growing in the water, the larva leaves the pond. It makes a small chamber for itself in the dirt at the pond's edge. Inside the chamber, the larva molts one more time and becomes a pupa. Underneath the old exoskeleton, a hard **pupal shell** has already developed.

Protected by this covering, the pupa will gradually change into an adult beetle.

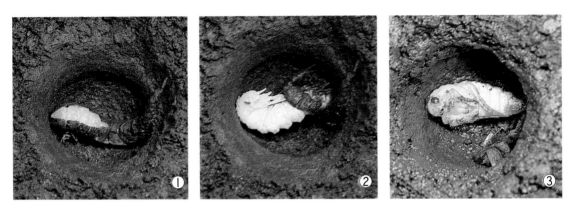

1) Four days after it enters the chamber, the larva begins to molt for the final time. 2) As the old exoskeleton is shed, the pupa is revealed. 3) Under the pupal shell, the body of the adult beetle begins to form.

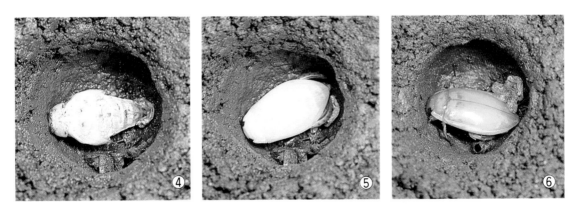

4) By the morning of the 12th day, the wings of the adult insect can be seen. The beetle's development is almost finished. 5) Twenty minutes later, the adult beetle is completely formed, but its body and wings are pure white. 6) After six more hours, the diving beetle has turned a yellowish color.

Nine hours after its development is finished, a predaceous diving beetle has a hard, brown body similar to the body of a full-grown adult. In a few more days, it will push its way out of the underground chamber and begin its life in the pond.

When winter comes to the pond, the lives of water insects undergo a great change.

SEASONS IN THE POND

Water insects usually complete their development and become adults in the summer. While the weather and the water in the pond are warm, they live active lives, moving around and hunting for food. When colder weather arrives, they must get ready for **hibernation.**

Hibernation is an inactive stage in an animal's life. While an insect is hibernating, its breathing, circulation, and other body systems slow down. This makes it possible for the insect to survive without food and with very little oxygen.

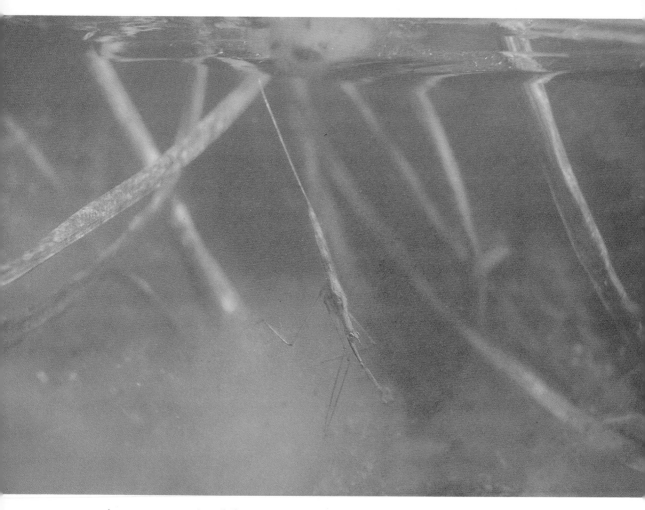

A water scorpion hibernating under the ice. Special chemicals in the insect's body keep it from freezing.

Water insects hibernate in different places. Some stay in the water or burrow into the mud at the bottom of the pond. Others leave the water and hide beneath rocks or plants on the shore. In these quiet places, they will wait until life returns to the pond in spring.

A giant water bug hibernating beneath a layer of straw. When winter is over, the insect will become active again. It will reproduce one more time before its life comes to an end.

GLOSSARY

exoskeleton—the tough outer covering of an insect's body that protects the internal organs and provides a framework for muscles

hibernation—a state of inactivity during which an animal's circulation, respiration, and other body systems slow down

larvae (LAR-vee)—the second stage in the development of beetles and many other insects. A larva is usually worm-like and lacks many of the body parts of an adult insect.

molting—shedding an old exoskeleton to make way for a new one

nymphs (NIMFS)—the second stage in the development of bugs and other insects such as grasshoppers and dragonflies. A nymph looks much like an adult insect of its species, with only a few body parts undeveloped.

plastron (PLAS-truhn)—a thin film of air held by hairs on the bodies of some water insects

predator—an animal that kills and eats other animals

prey—an animal that is killed and eaten by another animal

pupa (PEW-puh)—the third stage in the development of beetles and many other insects, during which the larva changes into an adult insect

pupal shell—the hard covering that protects the bodies of some insects during the pupal stage

respiratory (RES-pih-ruh-tor-ee) tubes—tubes on the abdomens of some water insects that are used to bring oxygen from the surface

spiracles (SPEAR-ih-kuhls)—air holes on the outside of an insect's body that are connected to a system of internal tubes

surface tension—a force that causes water to behave as if it were covered by a thin, elastic film. Surface tension is produced by attraction between the molecules in the upper layer of the water.

THE SCIENTIFIC NAMES OF WATER INSECTS

All the water insects described in this book belong to one of two different *orders* in the system of scientific classification. Beetles are members of the order Coleoptera, and bugs belong to the order Hemiptera. Within the system of classification, orders are broken up into smaller groups called *families*. Familes are further divided into groups known as *genera* (singular, *genus*). Finally, each genus is made up of one or more *species*, which is the basic group in the system of classification. Listed below you will find the family and genus names of the insects in the book, along with their common English names.

COLEOPTERA

Common English Name	Family	Genus
Predaceous diving beetle	Dytiscidae	*Cybister*
Whirligig beetle	Gyrinidae	*Gyrinus*
Water scavenger beetle	Hydrophilidae	*Hydrophilus*

HEMIPTERA

Common English Name	Family	Genus
Backswimmer	Notonectidae	*Notonecta*
Water strider	Gerridae	*Gerris*
Giant water bug	Belostomatidae	*Lethocerus*
Giant water bug	Belostomatidae	*Diplonychus*
Water scorpion	Nepidae	*Ranatra*
Water scorpion	Nepidae	*Laccotrepes*

INDEX